RULERS AND THEIR TIMES

QUEEN VICTORIA
and Nineteenth-Century England

by Claire Price-Groff

BENCHMARK BOOKS

MARSHALL CAVENDISH
NEW YORK

ACKNOWLEDGMENTS

With thanks to the members of the staff (especially Jeff)
of the Murphy, North Carolina, library for their generous help and
support. And to Professor Carl B. Estabrook of the Department of
History, Dartmouth College, Hanover, New Hampshire,
for his thoughtful reading of the manuscript.

With thanks, too, to Miriam Greenblatt, for originating
the idea for this series.

To my ninth-grade teacher, who taught me that history
is far more than lists of names and dates

Benchmark Books
Marshall Cavendish
99 White Plains Road
Tarrytown, New York 10591-9001
www.marshallcavendish.com

Library of Congress Cataloging-in-Publication Data
Price-Groff, Claire.
Queen Victoria and nineteenth-century England / by Claire Price-Groff.
p. cm. — (Rulers and their times)
Summary: Provides an overview of Queen Victoria's life and reign and of the daily lives of the people of
nineteenth-century England, and includes excerpts from letters, newspaper articles, and books of the time.
Includes bibliographical references (p.) and index.
ISBN 0-7614-1488-6
1. Great Britain—History—Victoria, 1837–1901. 2. Victoria, Queen of Great Britain, 1819–1901.
3. England—Social life and customs—19th century. 4. England—Social conditions—19th century.
5. Queens—Great Britain—Biography. [1. Great Britain—History—Victoria, 1837–1901. 2. Victoria,
Queen of Great Britain, 1819–1901. 3. England—Social life and customs—19th century. 4. England—
Social conditions—19th century. 5. Kings, queens, rulers, etc.] I. Title. II. Series.
DA550 .P85   2003   941.081—dc21   2002001095
Map by Rodica Prato
The author is grateful to Mercier Press and Patrick Conroy for permission to reprint the excerpt from
Robert Whyte's *Famine Ship Diary*.

Printed in Hong Kong
1 3 5 6 4 2
Photo research by Linda Sykes Picture Research, Hilton Head SC
Cover: Osborne House, London/AKG London; pages 5, 12, 21, 23, 40, 43, 44, 57, 60, 66, 81, 88: Mary
Evans Picture Library; pages 6–7: Windsor Castle, Royal Art Collection/AKG London; page 15: National
Museum of Art, Havana/AKG London; pages 18, 28: British Museum/Bridgeman Art Library; pages 25, 72:
Phillips, The International Fine Art Auctioneers, UK/Bridgeman Art Library; pages 31, 33: The FORBES
Magazine Collection/Bridgeman Art Library; pages 36–37: Gaetano Marzotto Collection/AKG London;
page 39: AKG London; pages 47, 74–75: Fine Art Photographic Library, London/Art Resource; page 48:
Roy Miles Gallery, London/Bridgeman Art Library; pages 50, 55, 63: Private Collection/Bridgeman Art
Library; pages 51 left, 51 right: Leeds Museums and Art Galleries/Bridgeman Art Library; page 53: Victoria
and Albert Museum, London/Art Resource; page 56: Yale Center for British Art, Paul Mellon
Collection/Bridgeman Art Library; page 69: Musee d'Orsay/AKG London

Contents

"I Will Be Good"

When Victoria, at eleven years old, realized she would be her country's next queen, she said, "I will be good." And throughout her long life, goodness is what she strived for.

Queen Victoria was not the kind of monarch who had the power to chop off heads or even to make her own laws. By the time she became queen, England was already a constitutional monarchy. The monarch was subject to the law of the land, or the constitution. England's constitution had developed slowly, over the centuries, and was an unwritten set of laws. Gradually, England's kings and queens had given over power to the upper and middle classes. By 1837, when Victoria became queen, most government policy was made by the prime minister and the lawmakers in Parliament, who were elected by a part of the populace. By the end of her long reign, in 1901, the queen had lost even more power and her role had become mainly ceremonial—but important, nonetheless.

Victoria wasn't particularly pleased with the changes in her position, but she learned to accept them. And it was her acceptance that helped Great Britain remain a constitutional monarchy while many other countries in Europe were overthrowing their kings and queens and becoming republics.

The world was changing quickly during Victoria's lifetime, thanks mainly to the Industrial Revolution. And while some people were enjoying the technological benefits the new era introduced, many

Victoria was queen of Great Britain for sixty-four years—the longest reign in English history.

felt insecure. They looked for something to anchor them, something that offered stability and comfort. It was there that Queen Victoria made her mark and her most lasting legacy. For Queen Victoria was an old-fashioned sort of person. She held traditional values and she liked stability. She was a wife and mother as well as a queen, and she was deeply involved in the lives of her nine children. She also set the tone for the period that was named for her—the Victorian Age.

PART ONE

Queen Victoria meets with the prime minister and other government officials. Although she was young and inexperienced when she became queen, Victoria took to her new role as if she had been ruling all her life.

England in the Victorian Age

The Richest Country in the World

When Victoria was born, England, a country smaller than the state of North Carolina, ruled a growing empire with territories in many parts of the world. Located to the northwest of continental Europe, this small country, along with Scotland and Wales, occupies an island roughly the size of the six New England states. Close by but separated by a stretch of ocean is Ireland, another island. Long ago, England took control of both islands. Together, they became the United Kingdom, or Great Britain.

By the 1500s Great Britain had already begun to look beyond its seas, and by the early 1600s it had established colonies in North America and the West Indies. By the end of Victoria's reign, three hundred years later, Britain had added many lands to its empire. It had colonies in Asia, Australia, New Zealand, the Pacific islands, India, Africa, and the Middle East. It was said that the sun never set on the British Empire.

Raw materials from the colonies were sent to England, where they were manufactured into goods that were traded back to the colonies and to other countries. This trade made England the richest country in the world in Victoria's day.

Queen Victoria saw many changes during her long reign. Many of these changes had begun with the Industrial Revolution, which

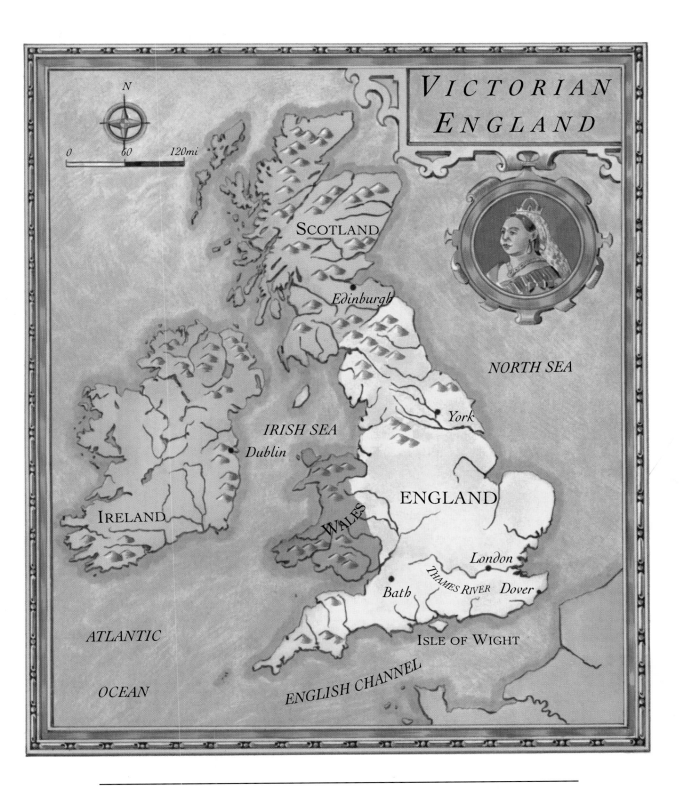

started in England in the eighteenth century and progressed rapidly under Victoria. Instead of producing goods by hand, products were made by power-driven machinery. Instead of working at home, people worked in factories. New inventions—from the steam engine to tin cans to telephones and motorcars—forever changed the way people lived and worked. Advances were made in medicine, too, and more people were able to live healthier and longer lives. In many ways life became better. But the changes benefited mostly the upper and middle classes—not the poor and working classes. While the well-to-do enjoyed unprecedented prosperity, the poor and working classes lived in great poverty.

These social inequities were perhaps the greatest challenge that Queen Victoria faced. How would she and her ministers cope with the call for reform from the "common people," who wanted greater opportunities for themselves and their children? Could there be change without radically overthrowing the old order? And would a young overprotected noblewoman know how to keep the balance?

Victoria's Early Years

When Victoria was born on May 24, 1819, few people thought she would ever become queen. True, she was the reigning king's only grandchild, but three uncles and her father stood ahead of her in the line of succession. Her father, Edward, duke of Kent, would become king only if he outlived all three of his older brothers—and then, only if none of them had children. And even then, Victoria would sit on the throne only after her father died.

But Edward and his wife, Princess Victoria Mary Louisa of Saxe-Coburg (a German state), had faith in the fortune-teller who had once told Edward that his daughter would be a great queen. So firmly did Edward believe this that, when Victoria was born, he said, "Take care of her for she will be Queen of England."

Victoria moved up the line of succession far more rapidly than her father could have imagined. Edward died of pneumonia when his infant daughter was only eight months old. A week later, Edward's father, King George III, who had reigned for many years, also died. Now only the new king, George IV, and his brothers Frederick and William were ahead of Victoria. Frederick died a few years later, moving Victoria up another notch.

Victoria was brought up by her mother, the duchess of Kent, in

Two-year-old Victoria poses with her mother, the duchess of Kent. The little princess is holding a portrait of her father, Edward, who died when she was a baby.

Kensington Palace, but she and her mother were not wealthy. Edward had died heavily in debt, and the duchess and Victoria were dependent on a small allowance granted them by King George IV and some assistance from the duchess's brother Leopold. So, although she was a princess and lived in a palace, Victoria had a far from luxurious life. Much later, she wrote, "We lived in a very simple plain manner. . . . Breakfast was at half past eight, luncheon at half past one, dinner at seven. . . . Tea was only allowed as a great treat in later years."

The duchess and George IV did not like each other. In fact, the duchess didn't like any of the royal brothers, all of whom had been involved in scandals and what she considered loose living. Because she didn't want Victoria influenced by her uncles, she kept her away from them.

Privately, the duchess hoped that both King George IV and his brother William, his successor, would die before Victoria reached her eighteenth birthday. If that happened, the duchess would be named regent—a person who acts for the monarch. Supporting her in this hope was her close friend John Conroy, whom she had named as her private secretary. The duchess and Conroy wanted to be the only people to influence Victoria.

Throughout her childhood, Victoria was allowed almost no contact with anyone other than her mother, Conroy, and Fräulein Louise Lehzen, her governess. Her only friends were her dolls and her dog. She slept in her mother's room, and never—not even once—was allowed a visitor without either her mother or Conroy present.

What Victoria thought of this no one knows, for the little girl had learned to keep her most private thoughts to herself.

Preparing To Be Queen

When Victoria was eleven years old, King George IV died, and her uncle William became king. Victoria had no idea what this meant to her. Then one day Fräulein Lehzen showed Victoria a chart that made it clear that the young girl would be England's next monarch. According to the governess, who wrote of this event years later, Victoria said, "I see I am nearer to the Throne than I thought. . . . I will be good!"

The year Victoria turned thirteen, the duchess and Conroy arranged annual tours around England to present her to her future subjects. Before her first trip, the duchess gave Victoria a diary, which began with this entry on July 31, 1832: "This Book Mamma gave me that I might write the journal of my journey to

King George IV ruled England for only ten years. As a young man, he had been admired for his cleverness and charming manners, but wild living and extravagance made him an unpopular king.

Wales in it." After a visit to a coal-mining district, Victoria wrote, "The men, women, children, country and houses are all black. . . . The grass is quite blasted and black. . . . Everywhere, smoking and burning coal heaps, intermingled with wretched huts and carts and little ragged children." Victoria probably did not record her most private thoughts in her diary because both her mother and her governess read it every night. However, once she formed the habit of keeping a diary, she kept it up for the rest of her life.

Victoria often corresponded with her uncle Leopold, who was the king of Belgium. His letters advised her on the duties of a queen: "The business of the highest in a State is certainly . . . to act with great impartiality and a spirit of justice for the good of all." He counseled her to be "courageous, firm, and honest."

As Victoria approached her eighteenth birthday, the duchess realized that her chance of becoming regent had passed. But she also knew that King William was ill and likely to die soon. She and Conroy repeatedly asked Victoria to name Conroy as her private secretary, an office that would give him—and through him, the duchess—considerable power once Victoria became queen. But as many times as they asked, Victoria, known for her stubbornness, resolutely refused.

In 1837, four weeks after her birthday, she wrote in her journal: "I was awoke at 6 o'clock by Mamma, who told me that the Archbishop of Canterbury and Lord Conyngham [the Lord Chamberlain] were here and wished to see me. I got out of bed and went into my sitting room . . . <u>alone</u> [without her mother], and saw them. Lord Conyngham then acquainted me that my poor Uncle, the King, was no more, and had expired at 12 minutes past 2 this morning and consequently that <u>I</u> am <u>Queen.</u>"

Her Majesty, the Queen

The very day she learned that she was queen, Victoria ordered her bed removed from her mother's room and had a servant inform the duchess that in the future, if she wanted to see Victoria, she had to make an appointment.

Later that day, she met with the prime minister and other high officials—"of COURSE quite ALONE as I shall always do all my Ministers." (Victoria often emphasized words in her diary with the use of capital letters and underlining.) The new monarch was, it seems, determined to be independent.

Until that day, Victoria had never had the slightest thing to do with government or politics. Everyone wondered what she would be like, this young inexperienced girl who had never been in a room without her mother. Her closest advisers, the members of her cabinet, may have expected to meet a shy, self-doubting girl who could be easily manipulated. If so, they were mightily surprised.

When Victoria met with the members of her cabinet for the first time, "She bowed to the Lords," as one member later wrote, "took her seat, and then read her speech in a clear, distinct, and audible voice, and without any appearance of fear or embarrassment."

Within days the new queen moved from Kensington to Buckingham Palace. Her mother and Conroy went with her, but

Victoria made sure her mother's apartment was set up in a different part of the palace from her own. Conroy maintained his position as the duchess's secretary.

The young queen thoroughly enjoyed both her newfound freedom and her position as monarch. Each day, accompanied by almost her entire court, she rode her horse through the vast parks surrounding the palace. At night, she reveled in rounds of parties and balls, dancing until dawn, then watching the sun rise.

But being a queen was more than parties and balls. There was a country to run, and although Parliament and the prime minister handled most government matters, Victoria was still the queen. She enjoyed the daily business of state as much as she did her royal diversions. "I have <u>so many</u> communications from the Ministers," she wrote. "I get so many papers to sign every day, that I have always a <u>very great</u> deal to do. I <u>delight</u> in this work."

Victoria became very close to Lord Melbourne, the prime minister, who acted as her teacher, adviser, and confidant on everything from English history to statecraft and her role as queen. She learned that power in England was continuing to shift. The small group of nobles who made up Britain's upper classes was continuing to lose power to the middle classes. The change could be seen in Parliament, where the House of Lords, comprised of titled nobility and high church officials, was losing power to the House of Commons, made up of elected representatives of the people.

Although the members of the House of Commons were elected, they did not represent all of the people, for not everyone could vote. Only men who owned property were enfranchised. Five years before Victoria became queen, Parliament had passed a

Patient and affectionate, Lord Melbourne became almost like a father to the young queen. The prime minister spent long hours with Victoria, playing games and doing puzzles, as well as lecturing her on politics and her duties as a constitutional monarch.

reform bill that reduced the amount of property a man had to own in order to vote. Many people were not satisfied with this new legislation. They wanted to see all property requirements removed. By the end of Victoria's reign, after the passage of two more reform bills, all adult working men—but no women—would have the vote. From then on, the House of Commons would have greater power than the House of Lords.

Victoria would not be happy with these changes, for her power as queen would have greatly diminished. But that was still a long way off, and the young monarch still had much to learn.

Some Hard Lessons

In 1839, two years after Victoria succeeded to the throne, the Whig party lost its control of Parliament, and Tory leader Robert Peel prepared to become prime minister. Victoria did not like Peel. She thought him a "cold, unfeeling, disagreeable man." When Peel asked the queen to replace some of her ladies-in-waiting, whose husbands were prominent Whigs, with women whose husbands were Tories, Victoria refused. She claimed that her ladies-in-waiting were members of her personal staff and not concerned with politics. Peel thought differently. He knew that he could never form an effective government if the queen's household was filled with ladies whose husbands were his strongest political opponents. Stubbornly, Victoria stood her ground. Without the support of the queen, Peel was forced to give up his efforts to establish a new government. The Whigs returned to power, along with their leader, Lord Melbourne. Victoria was delighted, but she was to fare worse in the next problem she faced.

As queen, she always insisted that every member of her court behave with propriety at all times. When Lady Flora Hastings, lady-in-waiting to Victoria's mother, was seen traveling in John Conroy's coach, Victoria suspected that the two were having a love affair. Later, when Lady Flora became noticeably heavier, Victoria accused her of carrying Conroy's child and dismissed Conroy from the royal household. When Lady Flora protested her innocence, Victoria demanded that she be examined by a doctor.

The doctor, a member of the court, confirmed Victoria's suspicions. However, Lady Flora went to another doctor who found that she was not pregnant but was suffering from cancer of the liver. Lady Flora's illness worsened and she died. People were angry with Victoria for her harsh treatment of the lady. The newspapers attacked her, and some people hissed when she appeared in public. Victoria felt "disgusted with everything." But the young queen would soon regain her popularity and find greater happiness than ever before.

A Royal Romance

Many people thought it was time for Victoria to marry. Victoria did not agree. As the world's most desirable "catch," she had many suitors and was enjoying herself too much to choose.

One of these suitors was her cousin Albert, whom she had met for the first time on her seventeenth birthday, three years earlier. Albert, a prince of the German state of Saxe-Coburg, was the son of a brother of Victoria's mother. Since the day of Albert's birth, three months after Victoria's, both families had hoped for a match. In the fall of 1839, Victoria agreed to meet him again but said that she would not consider marrying for at least another four years.

When she met Albert this time, however, she fell hopelessly in love. "Oh, when I look in those lovely, lovely blue eyes, I feel they are those of an angel," she wrote after their reunion. A few days later, she wrote that she was thinking seriously about marriage. And

Monarchs often marry for political reasons, but Victoria was deeply in love with Albert. At first the British people were unhappy with the German prince, but in time Albert's devotion to the queen and his concern for public affairs won him respect and popularity.

two days after that: "I sent for Albert; he came to the Closet [a monarch's private room] where I was alone. . . . I said to him, that it would make me <u>too happy</u> if he would consent to what I wished (to marry me). We embraced. . . . He said he would be very happy . . . and was so kind, and seemed so happy." Since Victoria was a queen, protocol demanded that the marriage proposal come from her, not Albert.

They married on February 10, 1840. Albert's position was a difficult one. In an age when husbands were considered the head of the household, Albert was definitely not the head of his. In all things, he was second to the queen. He lived in *her* country, in *her* home, with *her* furniture. And it was the queen who had a job, not he. When Albert suggested they take a leisurely honeymoon, Victoria told him, "I am the Sovereign, and that business can stop and wait for nothing. Parliament is sitting and something occurs almost every day for which I am required." She consented to a honeymoon of only three days.

While Victoria's journal reveals her deep love for her husband, it also shows that she feared having children. She knew that many women died in childbirth. She also disliked the smells and noises associated with babies. Despite her qualms, she became pregnant within a few weeks of the wedding. As her pregnancy progressed, Victoria found herself less able to cope with her official demands and turned some of them over to Albert.

A Model Family

In most royal marriages, extravagant living and adultery were not only practiced but flaunted. This had been especially true of

A noble visitor presents a gift for Prince Arthur, the seventh of Victoria and Albert's nine children. The royal couple were devoted parents who, said one historian, were "as happy playing Blind Man's Buff with the children as they were at the grandest opera."

Victoria's immediate predecessors. The young royal couple was determined to set a new standard—one of fidelity, propriety, and frugality. Family life would be treasured.

Their first child, Princess Victoria, was born in November 1840. Prince Albert Edward followed in 1841. Over the next eighteen years, seven more children were born to them. When the children were grown, they married into nearly all the royal houses of Europe, so that in the next generation Victoria was literally "Grandmama" to most of the princes and princesses of Europe.

And while the queen continued to be involved in state affairs, it was her family that was closest to her heart. She came especially to enjoy the times she, Albert, and the children spent away from London—at Osborne, their house on the Isle of Wight, and at Balmoral, the palace Albert designed in the Scottish Highlands.

New Laws and a Great Exhibit

Although Albert had no official role in the government, he was Victoria's private secretary and her closest adviser. It was largely thanks to his influence that Victoria learned to better understand her role as a constitutional monarch. He made her see that she should not publicly favor one party over the other but should work with whichever of the two main parties—the Whigs or the Tories—held the majority in the House of Commons. In 1841 the Whig party had again fallen from power, and this time Tory leader Robert Peel succeeded in becoming prime minister. Victoria still did not like Peel. But Albert persuaded her to agree to replace some of the Whigs in her household with Tories.

Albert also encouraged the queen to patronize, or support, young artists and architects. In 1851 he organized the Great Exhibition to show off the many new inventions of the times that helped improve the lives of ordinary people. To house his exhibition, Albert commissioned the building of a gigantic structure of iron and glass, known as the Crystal Palace. For six months, people from all parts of Britain—and the world—came to view displays of machinery, manufactured goods, and decorative arts from Britain and other countries. Included in the exhibits were locomotives, printing machines, textile machines,

The Crystal Palace exhibition has been called the first world's fair. Exhibits from all over the world filled the enormous hall, showcasing the inventions and advances of the Victorian Age.

the telegraph, furniture, porcelain, and tapestries.

"It was the <u>happiest, proudest</u> day in my life," Victoria noted in a letter to her uncle Leopold on the exhibition's opening day. "Albert's dearest name is immortalised with this <u>great</u> conception, <u>his</u> own, and my <u>own</u> dear country <u>showed</u> she was <u>worthy</u> of it."

It was also Albert's influence that made Victoria more aware of the hardships people of the working class were enduring and led her to support some of the legislation proposed in Parliament to help them. Laws were passed to fund and regulate free public education. A limit was placed on the number of hours a day women and children could be made to work in factories and mines. The Second Reform Act was enacted, further lowering property requirements for voter eligibility. These new laws did not solve all the problems, but they helped to alleviate the worst of them.

Troubles Abroad

The Crimean War

In the early 1850s, England joined the Ottoman Empire (now Turkey) in its war against Russia, hoping to protect British interests in the Middle East. Much of the fighting took place on the Crimean Peninsula (now part of Ukraine) in the Black Sea. The Crimean War was a bloody one, and thousands of British soldiers died, many from disease and infected wounds. Victoria applauded Florence Nightingale's new nursing methods and organized ladies' aid groups to help supply bandages and blankets. At the end of the war, the queen created a special medal, the Victoria Cross, which she personally awarded to many veterans.

The Indian Mutiny

The Crimean War had hardly ended when trouble erupted in India. Much of India had long been ruled not by the English government but by the British East India Company, a private English trading corporation, and by the British army. In 1857 resentment spread among Indian soldiers in the British army after they were issued a new cartridge for their rifles. The cartridge had to be bitten before it was loaded into the gun, and rumors spread that it was coated with the fat of cows (a sacred animal to Hindu soldiers)

To the Indian people, the Indian Mutiny of 1857–1858 is known as the First War for Independence. Thousands of Indian mutineers and British troops and civilians died in the bloody conflict.

and pigs (an unclean animal to Muslims). Rather than break a strong religious taboo, the soldiers rebelled, slaughtering hundreds of European men, women, and children in India. British reprisals were just as horrible. Victoria urged Parliament to order the army to quash the mutiny, but when this was accomplished, she advocated leniency toward the rebels. Control of India was then transferred from the British East India Company to the British government. India remained under British rule until after World War II.

Famine in Ireland

There were also troubles closer to home. In Ireland the failure of the potato crop, that country's main source of food and income, caused a great famine in the 1840s. More than a million people died from starvation. Although grain was imported from other countries in an effort to help, the Corn Laws,* which imposed taxes on imported grains, kept the prices higher than most people could afford. Thousands of Irish men, women, and children crowded into the lower decks of steamships to emigrate to America or Canada. Later, the Corn Laws were repealed, but too late to do much good.

*The term "corn" was used for all grains.

Shadow of Death

The year 1861 was not a good one for Victoria. Her mother died in March, and the queen grieved deeply for her. Also, throughout that year, Victoria worried about Albert's health, which had never been good.

In November, after returning from a visit to their son Edward, Albert became very ill. He died on December 14. Victoria was devastated and sank into a depression that lasted for several years. In a letter to her uncle Leopold she wrote, "The poor fatherless baby of eight months is now the utterly heartbroken and crushed widow of forty-two! My _life_ as a _happy_ one is _ended!_ The world is gone for _me!_ . . . I _had_ hoped with such instinctive certainty that God never _would_ part us, and would let us grow old together."

Victoria donned somber black mourning clothes, which she wore for the rest of her life. She kept Albert's rooms unchanged and insisted that fresh clothing be laid out on his bed every day. She refused to appear in public and performed only those royal duties that were absolutely necessary. For months, she even refused to open Parliament, a ceremony traditionally performed by the monarch. Over the next several years, she paid tribute to Albert's memory by erecting monuments and statues to him.

Life outside the palace continued during her long period of mourning. Both major political parties began to show greater concern for the welfare of working-class people. Laws were passed

After Albert's death Victoria put on black "widow's weeds" and wore them the rest of her life. Her long period of mourning earned her the nickname "Widow of Windsor."

to improve housing, education, and labor conditions. To rid themselves of their old images, both parties changed their names. The Whigs became the Liberal party, and the Tories became the Conservative party.

Outside Britain, the empire was expanding farther into Asia, Africa, and the South Pacific.

A Return to Public Life

Victoria slowly reentered public life. She was helped at first by her friendship with John Brown, a Scotsman who had been a member of Albert's staff. Later, she developed a close relationship with Benjamin Disraeli, who was elected prime minister on the Conservative ticket in 1868.

Victoria liked Disraeli's political views, which were similar to her own. Both of them wanted to continue to expand the already huge empire, and neither of them was in favor of any but the most basic social reforms. Opposed to Disraeli was William Gladstone, a Liberal, who thought the empire was large enough and that many more reforms were needed. Political power bounced between Disraeli and Gladstone for several years. Victoria had learned to work with whichever prime minister was in power, but she could never bring herself to like Gladstone. In 1876 Disraeli persuaded Parliament to pass the Royal Titles Act, which proclaimed Victoria "empress of India," much to her delight.

A few years later, in 1884, Parliament passed the last of the Reform Acts, extending the vote to all adult working men. Many women in Britain, like their sisters in America, also wanted the

Prime Minister Benjamin Disraeli's friendship and encouragement helped Victoria come out of her depression and return to public life. Disraeli was not only a powerful statesman but also a talented and witty novelist.

vote, but it would be a good many years in coming. Most members of Parliament were opposed to women's suffrage, as was the queen herself. She called it a "mad, wicked folly."

The End of an Era

In 1887, when Victoria had been queen for fifty years, the entire country celebrated her Golden Jubilee. By the time of her Diamond Jubilee, in 1897, honoring her sixtieth year as queen, Victoria was seventy-eight years old, yet she remained strong and continued to take an active interest in the affairs of the nation. Her dreams and Disraeli's had been realized. The empire had grown to the point where close to one-quarter of the world's population called her queen. It was an achievement of which she was understandably proud—and confident. When war threatened her empire, she was known to say, "We are not interested in the possibilities of defeat. They do not exist."

Only in the last year of her life did Victoria begin to show signs of weakness and old age. She died at Osborne on January 22, 1901, surrounded by her large family. With her last words, she called out to Albert.

Evaluating Victoria

The record of Victoria's life shows that she tried her best to fulfill her childhood vow of "I will be good," both as a monarch and a mother. Though her role in government lessened, she remained essential to her country and empire. During her sixty-five-year reign, she represented stability and security in a fast-changing world.

When she died, the entire empire mourned. Henry James, the nineteenth-century novelist, summed up her people's feelings when he wrote, "We all feel a bit motherless today: mysterious little Victoria is dead and fat vulgar Edward [her son] is king."

Not everyone admired her, however. One biographer criticized her for seeming "indifferent to, though possibly not unaware of, the plight of so many of her subjects." Yet on one point most historians agree: it was Victoria's commitment to duty, her sense of obligation to her country, and her acceptance of her role as a queen who ruled under a constitution that preserved the English monarchy.

PART TWO

London was a busy, bustling city in the Victorian Age, home to many thousands of people of all classes. Piccadilly Circus, lined with hotels, shops, and clubs, is still a center of traffic and amusement.

Everyday Life in Victorian England

The Industrial Revolution

Most revolutions are wars that overturn governments. The Industrial Revolution was not a war and did not overturn governments, but it did change life in every conceivable way. It began in the eighteenth century with the invention of the steam engine, which was used to run railroads, ships, and machinery. Other inventions followed, many of which were used in the factories that sprang up across the country in the nineteenth century.

When Victoria was born, the Industrial Revolution had yet to make its mark on the land. Most people still lived in rural areas. The main economy of the nation was farming and raising sheep. Land travel was limited to horse-drawn wagons or coaches, although most people walked to get where they wanted to go. Travel over water was by slow-moving barges or multimasted sailing ships. There were no telephones or telegraphs. There was no postal system—letters had to be conveyed by personal messenger.

By the time Victoria died, many people had left the farms to live in the thriving new industrial towns, where factories were producing textiles, cutlery, furniture, and other manufactured goods. Other people had moved to mining towns, where they labored underground to dig up the coal that powered the factories' machinery.

The steam engine transformed the worlds of transportation and industry. These ironworkers are marveling at the powerful new steam hammer, invented to forge parts for steamships and bridges.

The factory and mining towns soon grew into crowded cities. Factory owners built housing for their employees, but the homes were very close together, dreadfully small, and poorly constructed. Unsanitary conditions allowed diseases such as typhus and

Victorian Age "Firsts"

1800–1825
- Canned food
- Electric motor

1826–1850
- Transatlantic steamship crossing
- Chloroform used as anesthetic
- Chocolate bar
- Telegraph (perfected by Samuel Morse)
- Photography (invented by Louis Daguerre)
- Bicycle
- Indoor flushing toilet
- Zipper
- Saxophone
- Home sewing machine

1851–1875
- Can opener
- Transatlantic cable
- Submarine
- Underground railway (subway) in London
- Antiseptic surgery (introduced by Joseph Lister)
- Pasteurization and germ theory of infection (introduced by Louis Pasteur)
- Dynamite
- Electric dental drill
- Barbed wire
- Typewriter

1876–1900
- Telephone (invented by Alexander Graham Bell)
- Wireless telegraph (invented by Guglielmo Marconi)
- Contact lenses
- Light bulb and phonograph (invented by Thomas Edison)
- Electric tram
- Gasoline-powered automobile
- Pneumatic tire
- Primitive flying machine
- X rays
- Aspirin pills

London and Paris are linked by telephone in 1891.

cholera to flourish. Factory chimneys belched smoke and soot, which darkened the skies and blanketed everything, creating the bleak conditions recorded by thirteen-year-old Victoria during her annual tours of the countryside.

Transportation changed greatly in Victoria's lifetime. Railroads crisscrossed the land, from northernmost Scotland to Wales in the south. The railroads carried coal and raw materials to the factories and transported manufactured goods to shops. The locomotive also changed the way people traveled. Instead of depending on horse-drawn carriages and muddy roads, a traveler could now board a train and go many miles in comfort. Trips that were once considered great journeys were now easily accomplished.

Communication also got faster and faster. Mail was delivered through a well-organized postal system. Messages were tapped out on telegraph keys, sent, and received in minutes—even across the Atlantic Ocean. With the invention of the telephone, people could actually speak to one another over long distances. And by the end of the nineteenth century, early motorcars were chugging along newly built highways.

Life in London

London, England's capital and one of the largest cities in the world, was a fascinating place in Victoria's day. It teemed with life, high and low, rich and poor. Wealthy people lived in splendid town houses along the Thames River. Stately private dwellings for successful businessmen filled the suburbs that sprouted up on the outer edges of the city. Only a short distance away, in narrow alleys crowded with ramshackle hovels and dark tenements, the poor and working classes lived. Many of these people were former agricultural workers who had flocked to the city, hoping to find a better life. Most did not. They lived in terrible poverty, and many turned to crime.

In the center of the city, a multitude of shops lined the streets—tailors, drapers (fabric sellers), shoemakers, bakers, grocers, booksellers, stationers, milliners. Outside the shops, hawkers with pushcarts vied for customers, each trying to outshout the other: "Get the latest news here!" "Sweet oranges straight from Spain!" "Lovely posy for your lady!" "Hot eels. Have one, won't ye?" "Pint o' milk just a penny."

Shoeblacks, tinsmiths, and knife sharpeners offered on-the-spot repairs. Theaters and music halls provided entertainment. Pubs, taverns, and restaurants served food and drink. People conducted business in banks and offices.

Finely dressed ladies and gentlemen hurried along the crowded streets, past roughly dressed urchins and beggars. Barking dogs

Customers view the wares at a London grocer's shop. The manservant on the left is picking up a package for his master, while a grocer makes up another order for the seated woman and her curious boy.

darted between pedestrians and dodged wagon wheels, leaving their droppings behind them. Organ-grinders filled the air with music while their monkeys pranced about, begging for coins. And more than occasionally a pickpocket plied his or her trade, relieving people of purses, watches, and other valuables.

Other, more dangerous criminals thrived as well. Thieves broke

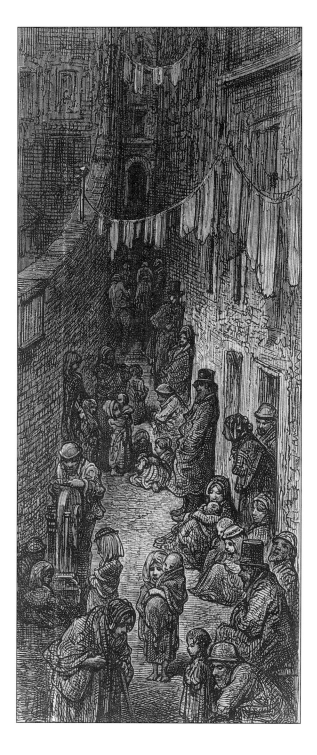

By the middle of the nineteenth century, more than half the people in England lived in cities. Many were crowded into foul slums, where sewage ran through the narrow alleys and sunlight rarely reached the ground.

into homes and shops. Pub brawls and street fights were common. People were attacked and murdered. Even serial murder was not unknown. In 1888 a criminal called Jack the Ripper brutally murdered several prostitutes. The case was never solved and has become part of English legend.

There was no real police force in London or anywhere else in Great Britain at the start of the nineteenth century. Often, criminals were pursued by private citizens, many of them paid as "watchers." Punishment was harsh and swift. Convicted criminals were hanged for all sorts of reasons, from murder and treason to burglary and small-time thievery. Until 1868 hangings were public spectacles and offered those with a taste for horror grisly entertainment.

In 1829 Robert Peel, then the home secretary, established London's first police force. (Police officers in England are still called "bobbies," after him.) As crime diminished somewhat, hanging was imposed only for murder, piracy, treason, or setting fire to an arsenal or dock. But punishment was still harsh. Criminals were publicly flogged or sentenced to walk the treadmill, a horrendous device made from a large wheel with steps. In another form of punishment, the criminal was forced to unwind endless yards of rope, strand by strand. The strands were then used to caulk ships. Deportation, either to Australia or New Zealand, was a common type of punishment, imposed for all sorts of crimes, including many that would be considered petty today.

Houses and Living Arrangements

The wealthiest Victorians lived in vast country manors, some with as many as thirty bedrooms. These enormous estates required a huge staff of servants to run them. Members of the lesser nobility and middle classes lived in more modest houses. The great majority of people in the country, the villagers, lived in small thatch-roofed cottages that were simply furnished, usually with just a table, a few chairs, and some straw pallets for sleeping.

In the cities a typical house for a middle-class family was tall and narrow. A small front lawn bordered with hedges shielded it from the street. A few steps led from the walkway up to the front door. Inside, a foyer, or reception hall, opened on to a drawing room on one side and a formal parlor and dining room on the other. Some houses featured a breakfast room as well. A staircase led up from the foyer to the second floor, which contained bedrooms for parents, older children, and guests. Young children slept in the nursery on the third floor, usually with their nurse or governess, while servants had small bedrooms in the attic. The kitchen was in the basement, reached indoors by a rear staircase and outside by a set of stairs leading down from the street. There might also be a separate scullery—a small washhouse—in the backyard, along with a kitchen garden and perhaps a stable or carriage house.

Wealthy Victorians often had homes in both London and the countryside. In this early nineteenth-century scene, an upper-class family takes tea on the lawn.

Furnishings

A narrow table, holding a silver dish for mail and visitors' calling cards, was often set against one wall in the foyer of the typical middle-class home. An umbrella stand, coatrack, and perhaps a straight-backed chair or two usually completed the reception area.

These simple furnishings were in marked contrast with the rest of the house, particularly the drawing room. It was here that the Victorians' passion for adornment was fully expressed. Collections of shells and fossils, bowls of waxed fruit, butterflies in glass cases, stuffed birds, miniature statues, photographs, and souvenirs from travels to the far reaches of the empire cluttered tabletops and

The sparkling Chinese porcelain, intricately woven Persian carpets, and handpainted furniture in this house—along with the owner's gorgeous clothes—all reflect the wealth of empire.

shelves. Glass-fronted cabinets held the family's most prized objects.

The drawing room furniture usually included a sofa and chairs, often in leather, which provided seating for guests who were entertained for afternoon tea or before and after dinner in the evening. The parlor, across the hall, reserved for more formal entertaining, was furnished with overstuffed sofas, silk or velvet upholstered chairs, and small carved-wood tables. A large dining table and chairs, sideboard, and china cabinet filled the dining room.

Oriental rugs with complicated patterns adorned the floors throughout the house, and walls were decorated with ornately framed family portraits suspended by long wires.

Bedrooms held metal-framed bedsteads, dark wooden dressers, and side tables. Often, a washstand with a large pitcher and basin served as a washing-up area, and a chamber pot under the bed took care of middle-of-the-night needs. Each bedroom had its own fireplace.

The kitchen had a stone floor, a large fireplace—or, later, a range—and a soapstone sink. A large wooden table in the center of the room provided work space.

Fireplaces, using wood or coal, were the only source of heat, but they were quite inefficient. Indoor plumbing, other than in the kitchen, was a luxury. For bathing, buckets of heated water were hauled up to the bedrooms by maids. By the middle of the century, indoor flush toilets had come into use, but there was usually only one for the entire household. Toilets were often placed in small enclosures in the backyard, because people were afraid that odors would foul their houses.

Keeping the House Clean

Victorians considered "cleanliness next to godliness," but keeping their homes clean was no easy task. Cooking and cleaning chores required much scrubbing, hauling, and just plain hard work. All those knickknacks and gewgaws had to be dusted and washed, rugs had to be beaten, silver had to be polished, fireplaces had to be cleaned, food had to be prepared and served, dishes had to be washed. Doing the laundry often took several days. First clothing

Toward the end of Victoria's reign, irons grew lighter. This household servant seems to be enjoying a quiet moment of reflection as she performs her task.

had to be soaked, boiled, scrubbed, rinsed, wrung out, and hung to dry. Then it had to be ironed—a big project, accomplished with coal-heated irons that weighed around ten pounds. Much of the clothing was made from heavy materials and was fashioned with intricate pleats and ruffles, which required meticulous ironing.

Who Did the Work?

The gentleman and lady of the house did little or none of this work. Well-to-do Victorians had a staff of servants: a butler to greet guests and perform personal services for the man of the house; a parlor maid to do light, general cleaning of the parlor, dining room, and drawing room; a housemaid to do heavy cleaning. Downstairs, the cook was in charge of the kitchen and often had scullery maids working under her. Children were looked after by a nanny or governess. Victorians who were not so well-off usually had at least a general maid of all work.

Middle- and upper-class Victorian households included a housekeeper, to oversee the other servants, and a coachman, to drive the family's coach, or carriage.

Housing for the Poor

Poor people, of course, had no luxuries whatsoever. In the cities they lived in tenements separated only by dark alleys. Entire families occupied one or two rooms, which were badly lightly and inadequately ventilated. Toilets were outhouses placed over open cesspits, emptied after dark by "night men." Water for cooking and bathing was drawn from a central outside tap or lugged from the river in buckets. Sewage from the cesspits often overflowed and ran into the unpaved streets. Needless to say, the rat population was almost uncontrollable and disease was widespread.

Family Life

Families of seven to nine children were common in Victorian England. Papa spent most of his time at work, leaving the care of the house and children to his wife. Papa always sat at the head of the table, carved the meat at dinner, and led the family in a before-dinner prayer. He was the boss of the house—not only of the children but of his wife as well. He made the rules, and everyone was expected to obey them. This was the way it was "supposed to be," but in many families, it was really Mama who made most of the household decisions.

In middle- and upper-class families, Mama was not expected to work—either in the house or outside. Her job was to supervise the servants and act as hostess at parties. In the afternoons she received lady visitors or called on other ladies for tea. She often kept busy by doing fancy needlework or, perhaps, by painting watercolors. She wasn't supposed to be interested in worldly affairs such as business or politics. Until late in the century, any money or property she had inherited from her father was controlled by her husband. She could not divorce her husband even if he beat her, but he could divorce her. If he did, the children remained with him. This changed in the 1870s and 1880s, when new laws gave women more rights.

Children were mostly cared for by a nurse or governess, who brought them down from the nursery in the afternoon for a visit

"Stick out your tongue," the little boy might be saying. A group of Victorian children play doctor in the parlor as a servant helps an elderly woman into the house.

with Mama. When they were around adults, children were expected to be seen and not heard, and to obey without question. Of course, this was the ideal, and not all children were always perfectly obedient.

Earning a Living

Members of the aristocracy seldom worked for a living. Their income came from the land and money they inherited. In England, under an ancient system known as primogeniture, the eldest son in a family inherited the entire estate. Younger sons had to seek their fortunes elsewhere and often entered the army or the clergy. Daughters were expected to marry and be supported by their husbands.

Middle-class men worked as lawyers, doctors, bankers, and craftsmen. Some owned factories, mills, and shops. Middle-class women who had to support themselves found that few occupations were open to them. They could become teachers or governesses. Or they could write. Although writing was one of the few occupations open to women, many published under men's names. George Eliot, the famous novelist, was really Mary Ann Evans. Other well-known nineteenth-century women writers were Elizabeth Barrett Browning, Jane Austen, and the Brontë sisters, Charlotte, Emily, and Anne. Later in the century, after women were admitted to universities, more job opportunities became available.

While women of the upper and middle classes were considered too delicate to work, working-class women were not. Many labored alongside the men in factories, textile mills, and coal mines. The hours were long. Working conditions were terrible, and the pay was poor.

Many working-class women labored fourteen hours a day, six days a week, in factories. The women in this textile mill work under a male foreman, tending the power looms that weave yarn into cloth.

Not all working-class people had jobs in factories and mills. Many were domestic servants, which allowed for little independence but provided a decent place to live and plenty of food. Many other men and women were self-employed. Cheapjacks sold small articles of hardware, watch chains, and knives from street stalls, calling out prices and bargains to attract customers. Costermongers hawked fruit, vegetables, and fish. Dustmen removed the ashes from peoples' fireplaces, then sold them to brick makers. Some women took in laundry and mending or worked as dressmakers at home. Packmen, lugging their wares in huge sacks on their backs, peddled cloth and small articles.

A muffin man trudges from one elegant London town house to the next, peddling his wares.

Piemen offered hot fruit or meat pies (rumored to be made from ground-up cat) as quick snacks. Rat catchers used ferrets to chase the ever-present rodents out of people's cellars. Once the rats were flushed out of their hidey-holes, small terriers caught them. There is a special breed of dog, the rat terrier, which today is a small pet but was originally bred to catch rats. Watermen, whose job required a seven-year apprenticeship, rowed people across the Thames or out to ships that were too large to anchor at a dock. Another kind of waterman, not so high on the social scale, provided water for the horses that drew cabs and carriages.

It wasn't only grown men and women who worked. Children joined the workforce as young as six or seven and were paid pennies a day for horrible jobs. One of the least terrible probably was that of "crossing sweeper": a young child would dodge in and out of the way of horses' hooves and carriage wheels, sweeping the mud from busy intersections so that ladies and gentlemen would not dirty their feet.

Much worse was the work of the "mudlarks," children between six and twelve who crept out onto the gunky banks of the Thames River at low tide, searching for pieces of coal, small coins, ends of rope, copper nails, and other debris that might later be sold.

Working-class children often worked long, hard hours in the mines, factories, or city streets. These boys dodge horses and carriages to earn a few pennies sweeping the crosswalks.

Some girls set up in business as "orange girls," selling fruit, along with bootlaces, corset laces, and other small articles. Others stood on street corners, selling a few matches for a penny. Perhaps one of the worst jobs for children was working as a chimney sweep's helper. Children between four and seven were perfect for this loathsome job because they were small enough to get inside a chimney to brush out a year's worth of accumulated soot and dust. Many young sweeps suffocated or fell to their deaths, and the job was so feared that little children were warned that if they weren't good, the "sweeps" would come and get them. The practice was outlawed shortly before Victoria became queen.

Working-class children who didn't work were left on their own or in the care of an older sister while their parents worked. Unlike middle-class youngsters, who were shielded from the harsher aspects of life, these children were exposed to all sorts of dangers, from crime to accident to disease.

Wages and Money

A well-paid bank clerk earned around 150 to 200 pounds a year, while business owners, bankers, lawyers, and doctors earned thousands. Many middle-class people earned as much in a day as a working-class family might earn in a year. An average working-class family earned between 1 $\frac{1}{2}$ and 2 pounds a week. The wages were not enough to keep up with their expenses and they were often in debt.

Many people who could not make a living left England, hoping to find a better life in Canada, the United States, Australia, or New Zealand.

What Victorians Ate

Middle-class and wealthy Victorians enjoyed a varied diet but, by modern standards, not a very healthy one. Meats accompanied by heavy sauces, overcooked vegetables, and rich desserts were served every day. Salads and raw vegetables were shunned as both unappetizing and unhealthy.

Poor people, however, could not afford this rich diet and subsisted mainly on porridge made from oats and barley or on soups made from cabbage, turnips, and potatoes. They also ate a lot of cheese and bread. Meat was a special treat reserved for holidays.

Cheap ale and beer were drunk by both children and adults. Few people drank water or milk, as both were often contaminated.

A Taste for Dining

Food and mealtimes were important to Victorians. People didn't rush through their meals as we do today—they liked to dine, not just eat. While the lady of the house planned the menus, her cook and kitchen staff purchased, prepared, and served the food. Many items were bought from the tradesmen—the butcher, the baker, the greengrocer, the milkman—who came knocking at the kitchen door.

Keeping food fresh was a big problem in a time before refrigerators and freezers. Many foods were preserved by salting, pickling, or smoking. It was not uncommon to see legs of mutton

Three generations of an upper-class Victorian family parade downstairs to a "simple" family meal.

(sheep meat), rounds of ham, and other meats hanging from kitchen rafters.

Breakfast in many households was huge. The table was loaded with cold sliced meats, meat pies, chops of mutton, steak, kidneys, bacon, eggs, toast, marmalade, tea, and coffee.

Cold meat and chops were eaten again at midday for lunch, perhaps with fruit and cakes for dessert. Men who worked in the city ate their lunch at a gentleman's club.

While breakfast and lunch were informal and often served in the breakfast room, dinner always took place in the dining room. There were several courses. First came a soup, followed by a large roast, potatoes, and boiled vegetables. Fish or chicken dishes might come next. Fruits and sweets finished off the repast.

Older children ate in the dining room with their parents, but younger ones had their dinner earlier in the nursery. Servants dined on leftovers in the kitchen after the family had been served.

Family dinners were simple affairs compared with the lavish dinner parties that Victorians enjoying having. A formal dinner could have as many as ten different courses plus dessert and coffee. Menus were set at each person's place, along with several plates and glasses, and silverware for each course. Maids or footmen served each guest from large platters. A different wine was offered with each course. During the meal, the guests engaged in polite—never controversial or serious—conversation.

After dessert, the ladies withdrew to the drawing room for tea while the men remained in the dining room to enjoy a cigar and a glass of port wine. Later, they joined the ladies for some more polite conversation.

Getting an Education

Benjamin Disraeli, one of Queen Victoria's favorite prime ministers, once said that England was "two nations [the rich and the poor] . . . who are as ignorant of each other's habits, thoughts, and feelings as if they were dwellers in different zones, or inhabitants of different planets." Nowhere was this truer than in the field of education. For much of the century, most children of the poor received no education at all.

Queen Victoria echoed the feelings of many in the upper classes who believed that educating the poor was dangerous. Once poor people had some schooling, it was thought, they might want more of a say in how the country was run. They might want to make laws that would improve their lives. No, much better to keep the poor uneducated.

The few schools that were available for poor children were run by ill-trained teachers and had little in the way of books or supplies. Dame schools, run by women from their homes, were more like day care centers than schools. Toward the middle of the century, some instruction in basic reading, writing, and arithmetic was provided by charity groups, churches, and even some factory owners.

Compulsory education was not established until 1870. Even then, it was only for children up to age ten, and many people continued to send their children to work instead of school because they needed the wages they earned.

The Apprentice System

Often, boys of poor and working-class parents were apprenticed out to learn a craft or trade. The apprentice lived with his "master," and was expected to do whatever he was told. He received no pay but was given room and board and, sometimes, small amounts of pocket money. If a boy was lucky, he was assigned to a kind

A young wig maker's apprentice practices his trade. Apprentices worked hard and were sometimes mistreated by their masters, but in the days before widespread public education, the system gave boys a chance to learn skills that would support them all their lives.

master who did not take advantage of him. Apprentices might train to become soap or candle makers, shoemakers, milliners, weavers, or silver- or goldsmiths. Not all worked for small, independent business owners. Some apprentices worked in huge factories or mills. Some also trained as law clerks, bank clerks, surgeons, or shopkeepers.

Young girls of working-class parents were often sent out as live-in house or scullery maids. This, too, was a sort of apprenticeship since the girl could work her way up to a higher position in the household.

Schools

Children of middle-class parents were taught by their nurse until they were around six or seven. Then boys were sent to boarding school, where they learned Latin and Greek literature and grammar, mathematics, logic and rhetoric (public speaking), history, and geography. Their schooling prepared them for entry into a university if they wished to continue their education.

Since the only thing girls were expected to do was find a suitable husband, get married, and have children, it was thought they had no need of formal education. They were tutored by governesses who read literature with them but mostly taught them how to be proper young ladies. They learned how to sew, sing, and play the piano, and how to conduct themselves in polite society.

Later in the century, more girls attended school, but even then, they were not expected to go to a university. In fact, no university would admit them. Only late in the century did universities start to open their doors to women.

Clothing and Fashion

Impossibly tiny waists, wide swaying skirts, and full bosoms were "the look" for women for most of the nineteenth century. To achieve this look, ladies wore long corsets stiffened with whale-bone inserts and tied in the back with lacings that molded their bodies into the required shape. A wire-hoop crinoline and layers of lacy petticoats were dropped over the corset to swish and sway under the wide skirt, which was topped with a tight-fitting bodice.

Extreme modesty was a hallmark of Victorian dress. A woman was not supposed to show any portion of her leg above her ankle. Daytime dresses had long sleeves and high necks. For evening, how-ever, low scooped necklines and short sleeves, worn with long gloves to cover the arms above the elbow, were considered fashionable.

Women dressed in this fashion looked romantic, but their corsets were laced so tightly they could take only shallow breaths. Also, many women's rib cages were permanently disfigured by being so tightly bound. Aside from the health problems they suf-fered by forcing their bodies into an unnatural shape, women had to struggle to get their wide skirts through narrow doorways and other tight spaces.

After the middle of the century, several individuals and groups campaigned against these ridiculous fashions. Eventually corsets

At the beginning of the Victorian Age, fashionable ladies were walking monuments of wire and whalebone. In this illustration from a story titled "Cupid and the Crinoline," the young man looks less than pleased with the outfit that will keep him at arm's length from his beloved.

were loosened a bit and crinolines and wide skirts were replaced with close-fitting ones. However, the narrow skirts were often adorned in the back with a huge bustle, so sitting comfortably was still a problem.

No well-dressed woman ventured outside without her gloves, her bonnet, and her parasol to protect her against the sun. Many bonnets were so large and lavishly decorated, with huge plumes of ostrich feathers, intricate folds of lace, imitation fruit and flowers, even stuffed birds, that they were ludicrous.

Like many of her subjects, Queen Victoria enjoyed wearing dresses of bright colors and prints when she was young. But when she switched to black dresses and simple, close-fitting bonnets after Prince Albert died, older women and widows followed her example.

Properly attired Victorian men wore striped trousers held in place by a strap that went under their shoes, white shirts with stiff collars, and cravats (wide ties). A checkered or plaid waistcoat (vest) and a frock coat that came down to the knees, a bowler or top hat, and a walking stick or umbrella completed the outfit. Most men sported a beard or mustache.

Both boys and girls wore loose-fitting dresses until they were around three years old. After that, girls were dressed as miniature women and boys as miniature men.

Science and Religion

A person's health was far more precarious in the nineteenth century than it is today. Many women died in childbirth, along with their infants. And many children who survived infancy died from diseases such as typhoid, cholera, or influenza before they reached the age of ten. These diseases also claimed the lives of grown men and women.

Most doctors continued to use methods inherited from medieval times, such as bleeding (cutting a vein and taking a quantity of blood) and leeching (placing live leeches on wounds to draw out blood). While most patients believed these treatments were effective, they probably killed more people than they cured. Surgery was performed with unsterile instruments and with anesthetics that were both ineffective and dangerous.

However, as the century progressed, things improved. Louis Pasteur, a French scientist, introduced the theory that disease was spread by germs. He also developed pasteurization, a method of sterilizing milk. Joseph Lister, a British surgeon, discovered the importance of antiseptic methods of surgery, and Florence Nightingale, the famous British nurse, taught other nurses how to keep wounds sterile. Vaccines were developed to immunize people against certain diseases. Better anesthetics were invented, along

Louis Pasteur's discovery that germs cause disease led to better sanitation and medical care. The French chemist spent much of his life working to eliminate the diseases that plagued people and animals, and succeeded in developing vaccines to prevent rabies and anthrax.

with the stethoscope. The discovery of radium led to the use of X rays as a diagnostic tool. All this new knowledge and technology greatly improved people's health and extended life expectancy.

Charles Darwin

Although most people in nineteenth-century England professed a profound belief in God, some began to question whether biblical events happened exactly the way the Bible said they did. Much of this questioning came about after Charles Darwin published his famous book *The Origin of Species,* in which he stated that all life on earth—plants, animals, and people—evolved from earlier forms. While some Victorians accepted Darwin's ideas, others were horrified by them, especially his theory that both people and monkeys were primates that had evolved from a common ancestor. Even today, some people still challenge the theory of evolution. However, nearly every scientist and most educated people accept that evolution is a fact.

Fun and Games

The Victorians had no movies, televisions, VCRs, computers, or electronic games; nonetheless they found many ways to amuse themselves. They attended the theater, screamed their lungs out at horse races, and enjoyed strolling along city streets and through the countryside. Much of their entertainment, though, was found at home. After dinner, everyone gathered in the drawing room while one family member read a chapter from the current best-seller, or perhaps the latest installment of a Sherlock Holmes mystery from a literary magazine.

When the family entertained visitors, charades and word games were enjoyed. Or they had musical evenings, playing the piano and other instruments and singing. Toward the end of the century, people might play records on Thomas Edison's new phonograph. Since photography was still fairly new, people also enjoyed posing for portraits.

Sports such as squash, rugby, croquet, and lawn tennis were popular. Team rowing was also fashionable and big regattas were regularly held on the Thames. Bicycling was a trendy sport for women, although how they managed this with their voluminous crinolines remains a mystery. The more daring women borrowed the new fashion of bloomer-trousers introduced in the United States.

Children of the wealthy and middle classes played with hoops, balls, and toy bow and arrows. Girls made tea parties for their

During quiet evenings at home, the lady of the house might entertain the family with her musical talents. The young woman in the background is a nursery maid, who has brought these well-mannered children down from the nursery for a visit with their parents.

dolls, while boys played war with lines of tin soldiers. Some toys were quite elaborate, such as intricate music boxes and miniature train sets. Rocking horses with real horsehair tails and manes were particularly popular.

Just as adults enjoyed reading, so did children. Some of the most popular books, such as *Alice's Adventures in Wonderland*, the stories of Hans Christian Andersen, and *Black Beauty*, are still enjoyed by children today. But many Victorian children's books would be considered a bit stuffy and preachy now. Some were pretty chilling as well, such as *The Little Matchgirl*, a story about a little girl who froze to death while selling matches in a midwinter storm.

While wealthy and middle-class people had plenty of time to enjoy these entertainments, most members of the working class had little opportunity for fun. Their children did not have the toys and books of the wealthy, but they still played, as children always do. They chased one another in tag and other street games. They also played soccer. Soccer was actually started by boys at English public schools and later became popular as an organized sport.

Special Days

Christmas—a favorite English holiday—was celebrated with caroling, visiting friends, and the new fashion of setting up Christmas trees, introduced by Prince Albert. He brought the tradition from his native Germany. Christmas celebrations, which included Boxing Day, the first weekday after December 25, continued until Twelfth Night on January 6.

On Valentine's Day, men and women sent elaborate handmade cards. Sometimes the sender was shy and sent the card from a "secret admirer."

In spring and fall, people enjoyed country fairs and festivals. Many villages continued the old pagan ceremony of dancing around a maypole on May Day.

PART THREE

First-class passengers traveled in style and comfort on the new railroads.

The Victorians in
Their Own Words

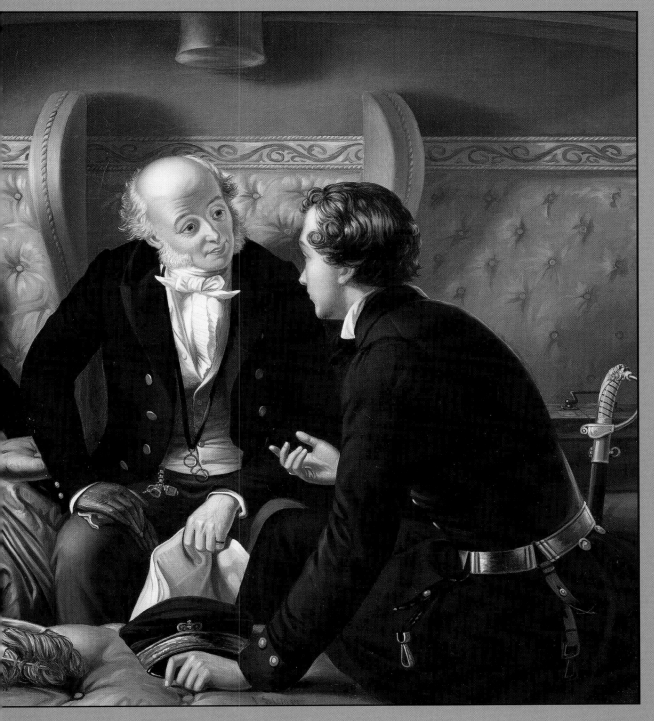

Rail travel was new and exciting in the nineteenth century. In this poem the famous Victorian author and poet Robert Louis Stevenson describes what a child may have felt as a train whisked him through the countryside:

From a Railway Carriage

Faster than fairies, faster than witches,
Bridges and houses, hedges and ditches;
And charging along like troops in a battle
All through the meadows the horses and cattle:
All of the sights of the hill and the plain
Fly as thick as driving rain;
And ever again, in the wink of an eye,
Painted stations whistle by.
Here is a child who clambers and scrambles,
All by himself and gathering brambles;
Here is a tramp who stands and gazes,
And there is the green for stringing the daisies;
Here is a cart run away in the road
Lumping along with man and load;
And here is a mill, and there is a river:
Each a glimpse and gone forever!

For many young people, the chance to work in one of England's colonies may have seemed like an excellent opportunity for adventure. This excerpt from an article in *Punch,* a popular magazine in Victoria's day, pokes fun at some of the advertisements companies placed to entice workers abroad:

Planters and Their "Plants"

Start in Life! A Ceylon Tea-Planter has vacancies for half-a-dozen young men on his small and miserably-unhealthy estate in the interior, which, except for the exorbitant premiums which he asks with each pupil, would probably go into the Bankruptcy Court to-morrow. They will gain practical experience of the minutiae [small details] of tea-growing, cholera, and jungle-fever. A year spent in this way may lead to a fortune; it may also lead to the local cemetery. A good place for a medical student wanting to study bacilli [bacteria], or for a coroner in search of active occupation. Delicate English youths come here, and leave in an incredibly short space of time with a wonderful knowledge of tea and no liver whatever. This is a chance which may never occur again.

Well over a million Irish people died from starvation and disease during the Great Potato Famine that began in 1845 and lasted for almost five years. Those who could—hundreds of thousands—escaped by emigrating to Canada or the United States. Most sailed the cheapest way possible, crowded together in the lower decks of ships as steerage passengers.

Many people thought the English government could have done more to help by providing more aid in Ireland and by better regulating conditions on the emigrant ships. This editorial from the London *Times* calls for a parliamentary investigation:

Friday, September 17, 1847:

More than a hundred thousand souls [flew] from the very midst of the calamity into insufficient vessels, scrambling for a footing on a deck and a berth in a hold, committing themselves to these worse than prisons, while their frames were wasted with ill-fare and their blood infected with disease, fighting for months of unutterable wretchedness against the elements without and pestilence within, giving almost hourly victims to the deep, landing at length on shores already terrified and diseased, consigned to encampments of the dying and of the dead, spreading death wherever they roam, and having no other prospect before them than a long continuance of these horrors in a still farther flight across forests and lakes under a Canadian sun and a Canadian frost. . . .

By the end of the season there is little doubt that the immigration into Canada alone will have amounted to 100,000; nearly all from Ireland. . . . The worst horrors of the slave trade which it is the boast of the ambition of this empire to suppress at any cost have been re-enacted in the flight of British subjects from their native shores. . . .

Historians and politicians will some day sift and weigh

the conflicting narrations and documents of this lamentable year, and pronounce, with or without affectation, how much is due to the inclemency [unmercifulness] of heaven, and how much to the cruelty, heartlessness or improvidence [unpreparedness] of man. The boasted institutions and spirit of this empire are on trial. They are weighed in the balance. Famine and pestilence are at the gates, and a conscience-stricken nation might almost fear to see the "writing on the wall." We are forced to confess that whether it be the fault of our own laws or our men, this new act in the terrible drama has not been met as humanity and common sense would enjoin. . . .

In the first place, our usual regulations as to the proportions of passengers to tonnage are lax enough. Then, it appears that British vessels bound to Canada, owing to the recent repeal of a former enactment, need not, and do not, take out surgeons. Then, as a correspondent informs us, the inspectors appointed to see that emigrant ships chartered from British ports observed such regulations as there are, have generally failed in their duty. Into this part of the business we hope that Parliament will not omit to inquire.

The lot of the emigrant, no matter what his or her social status, is difficult. It is always painful to leave the home where one was raised and all that is familiar for life in a strange new land. In the following diary entry, Robert Whyte, an Irishman, describes his experiences onboard an emigrant ship in 1847. He was one of the more fortunate travelers; unlike so many who rode in steerage, he had a first-class cabin:

> *Many and deep are the wounds that the sensitive heart inflicts upon its possessor, as he journeys through life's pilgrimage but on few occasions are they so acutely felt as when one is about to part from those who formed a portion of his existence; deeper still pierces the pang as the idea presents itself that the separation may be for ever, but when one feels a father's nervous grasp, a dear sister's tender, sobbing embrace and the eye wanders around the apartment, drinking in each familiar object, until it rests upon the vacant chair which she who nursed his helpless infancy was wont to occupy, then the agony he wishes to conceal becomes insupportable. . . .*
>
> *Tuesday, 1 June*
> *After breakfast, the mate invited me to see the depot of provisions. . . .*
> *By the light from the lantern I perceived a number of sacks, which were filled with oatmeal and biscuit. . . . I sat down upon one of the sacks, from beneath which suddenly issued a groan. I jumped up, quite at a loss to account for the strange sound and looked at the mate in order to discover what he thought of it. He seemed somewhat surprised but in a moment removed two or three*

Steerage passengers on a transatlantic crossing ride out rough seas on a ship's unsheltered deck.

sacks and lo! there was a man crouched up in a corner. As he had not seen him before, the mate at once concluded that he was a "stowaway," so giving him a shake to make him stand upright, he ordered him to mount the ladder, bestowing a kick upon the poor wretch to accelerate his tardy ascent.

The captain was summoned from below and a council immediately held for the trial of the prisoner. . . . He had been concealed for three days. . . . He had no clothes but the rags he wore nor had he any provisions. To decide what was to be done with him was now the consideration, but the captain hastily terminated the deliberation by swearing that he should be thrown overboard. The wretched creature was quite discomfited [disturbed] by the captain's wrath and earnestly begged for forgiveness. It was eventually settled that he should be landed upon the first island at which we should touch, with which decision he appeared to be quite satisfied. He said that he was willing to work for his support but the captain swore determinedly that he should not taste one pound of the ship's provision. He was therefore left to the tender mercies of his fellow passengers.

In consequence of this discovery, there was a general muster in the afternoon, affording me an opportunity of seeing all the emigrants—and a more motley crowd I never beheld; of all ages, from the infant to the feeble grandsire and withered crone.

While they were on deck, the hold was searched, but without any further discovery, no one having been found below but a boy who was unable to leave his berth from debility [weakness].

Thursday, 3 June

. . . The passengers' fireplaces, upon either side of the foredeck furnished endless scenes, sometimes of noisy merriment, at others of quarrels. The fire was contained in a large wooden case lined with bricks . . . the coals being confined by two or three iron bars in front. From morning till evening they were surrounded by groups of men, women and children; some making stirabout in all kinds of vessels, and others baking cakes upon extemporary [makeshift] *griddles. These cakes were generally about two inches thick, and when baked were encased in a burnt crust coated with smoke, being actually raw in the centre. Such was the unvaried food of the greater number of these poor creatures. A few of them, who seemed to be better off, had herrings or bacon. The meal* [coarsely ground grain] *with which they were provided was of very bad quality—this they had five days and biscuit, which was good, two days in the week.*

Books of etiquette were popular in Victorian England. They offered advice and guidance on proper behavior. Here are some excerpts from one of them, called *Youth's Educator for Home and Society:*

MANNERS NECESSARY TO GOOD STANDING

A rude, loud-spoken, uncultured woman is a positive blot upon nature. . . . A lady should be quiet in her manners, natural and unassuming in her language, careful to wound no one's feelings, but giving generously and freely from the treasures of her pure mind to her friends . . . having a gentle pity for the unfortunate, the inferior and the ignorant, at the same time carrying herself with an innocence and single-heartedness which disarms ill nature, and wins respect and love from all.

PRESENTING THE YOUNGER TO THE ELDER

When there is a marked difference in age, the younger lady should be presented to the elder lady, unless a superiority exists in position. . . . The unknown lady should be presented to the famous one. A gentleman is introduced to a lady. But as we have said elsewhere, it is unwise to be too ready to give introductions.

INTRODUCTION BY CARD

Introductions may be made by card as well as by letter. The gentleman introducing the other writes upon the upper left hand corner of his own card the words "Introducing Mr._____," and incloses [English spelling] *it with the card of the gentleman so named in an envelope of good quality, and of fashionable style and size. . . .*

    Etiquette declares that these rules be observed with unvarying exactness. Should the person introduced be a lady, she follows the same method of inclosing her card with that of the one introducing her, and sends it by mail or a messenger. The lady receiving these must call in person, or some member of her family must represent her. If she fails in this, she must send a message explaining her reason. Three days are the limit allowed for a call to be made, and if not made within a few days such an omission is an act of rudeness.

Victorians didn't have the convenience of refrigeration. They couldn't reach into the refrigerator for a cold can of soda or juice, or store a side of beef to keep it fresh before cooking. Here are two recipes from Victorian cookbooks that didn't require refrigeration. You may want to try making this nonalcoholic ginger beer, but the mutton roast might best be avoided:

ENGLISH GINGER BEER

Pour four quarts of boiling water, upon an ounce and a half of ginger, an ounce of cream of tartar, a pound of clean brown sugar, and two fresh lemons, sliced thin. It should be wrought [left standing] *twenty-four hours, with two gills* [ten ounces] *of good yeast, and then bottled. It improves by keeping several weeks, unless the weather is hot, and it is an excellent beverage.* [The yeast would have fermented the beverage, giving it a bit of carbonation and a slightly bitter taste.]

Roast Haunch of Mutton [LARGE ROAST OF SHEEP MEAT]
Ingredients: Haunch of mutton, a little salt, flour.
Mode: Let this joint [the haunch] *hang as long as possible without becoming tainted* [spoiled], *and while hanging dust flour over it, which keeps off the flies, and prevents the air from getting to it. If not well hung, the joint, when it comes to table, will neither do credit to the butcher or the cook, as it will not be tender. Wash the outside well, lest it should have a bad flavor from keeping; then flour it and put it down to a nice brisk fire, at some distance, so that it may gradually warm through. Keep continually basting, and about 1/2 hour before it is served, draw it nearer to the fire to get nicely brown. Sprinkle a little fine salt over the meat, pour off the dripping, add a little boiling water slightly salted, and strain this over the joint. Place a paper ruche* [ruffle] *on the bone, and send red-currant jelly and gravy in a tureen to table with it.*
Time: About 4 hours.
Seasonable: In best season from September to March.
Sufficient for 8 to 10 persons

In the early 1830s, Parliament made several investigations into working conditions for children in factories and mines. Testimony was presented by children currently employed, adults who had been employed as children, parents of employed children, medical examiners, factory owners, and others. As a result of these inquiries, Parliament passed the Factory Act of 1833, which limited the hours of employment for children. Before this law was enacted, children often worked as much as sixteen hours a day.

Testimony of Elizabeth Bently, age twenty-three, who began working in a flax mill at age six:

What was your business in the mill?
I was a little doffer.

What were your hours of labour in that mill?
From 5 in the morning till 9 at night, when they were thronged [very busy].

For how long a time together have you worked that excessive length of time?
For about half a year.

What were your usual hours when you were not so thronged?
From 6 in the morning till 7 at night.

What time was allowed for your meals?
Forty minutes at noon.

Had you any time to get your breakfast or drinking?
No, we got it as we could.

And when your work was bad, you had hardly any time to eat it at all?
No; we were obliged to leave it or take it home, and when we did not take it, the overlooker took it, and gave it to his pigs.

Do you consider doffing a laborious employment?
Yes.

Explain what it is you had to do.
When the frames are full, they have to stop the frames, and take the flyers off, and take the full bobbins off, and carry them to the roller; and then put empty ones on, and set the frame going again. . . .

Two barefoot young girls labor in a brickyard. Before Parliament passed laws protecting children, they worked for long hours at back-breaking, often dangerous jobs.

Suppose you flagged [slowed down] a little, or were too late, what would they do?

Strap [beat] *us.*

Are they in the habit of strapping those who are last in doffing?

Yes. . . .

Have you ever been strapped?

Yes.

Severely?

Yes.

[The examiner asked her what time she awoke to get to work on time. The young woman said that her mother sometimes woke her before 2:00 A.M.]

I have sometimes been at Hunslet Car at 2 o'clock in the morning, when it was streaming down with rain, and we have had to stay until the mill was opened.

Important Events in Nineteenth-Century England

1820s
- Robert Peel establishes first official London police force.

1830s
- Railroad connection between Manchester and Liverpool in England is completed.
- Slavery is abolished throughout British Empire.

1840s
- Penny post is established in England.
- Factory Act of 1847 limits working hours for women and children to ten hours a day.
- Failure of potato crop in Ireland causes Great Potato Famine.
- Revolutionary movement grows in Ireland to end English rule.

1850s
- Gold is discovered in Australia, resulting in wave of immigration.
- Charles Dickens's book *Hard Times* depicts terrible conditions in England's industrial towns.
- Charles Darwin's book *The Origin of Species* creates great controversy between science and religion.

- Police forces are established for every British county.
- First transatlantic cable is completed.

1860s
- A national association of trade unions is formed.

1870s
- First college for women is opened.
- Women are admitted to London University.
- People can vote with secret ballot.
- Children under age nine are prohibited from working in factories.
- Women begin to gain right to control their own money and property.
- Women are admitted to medical school.
- Workers have right to strike and make peaceful demonstrations.

1880s
- Free compulsory education is established for children to age ten.
- Vote is extended to all working men (but no women).

Glossary

anesthetic: A substance that is given to a patient so that no pain is felt during a procedure such as surgery.

antiseptic method: The practice of keeping sterile conditions during childbirth and surgery.

cabinet: A group of advisers to the head of a government.

controversial: Causing disagreement or arguments.

fräulein: An unmarried German woman; a German governess.

House of Commons: The more powerful of the two legislative bodies of the British Parliament; today the House of Commons is made up of 651 members, who are elected every five years.

House of Lords: One of the two legislative bodies of the British Parliament; the House of Lords is made up of members of the nobility and high church officials.

immunize: To protect against disease, usually with a vaccine.

milliner: Someone who makes and sells women's hats.

nobility: The uppermost class of British society, made up of people holding inherited titles.

Parliament: The legislative assembly of Great Britain, which includes the House of Commons and the House of Lords.

prime minister: The head of the British government (the monarch is the head of state). The prime minister is the leader of the political party with the most members in the House of Commons.

propriety: Behavior that is considered proper and respectable.

protocol: An official code of behavior.

pub: A public establishment where food and drinks are sold; a bar and restaurant.

scullery: A room for cleaning and storing dishes and cooking utensils and for doing messy kitchen work.

sideboard: A piece of furniture designed to store dishes and silverware.

steerage: A section of inferior rooms in a ship, set aside for the lowest-paying passengers.

tenement: A large apartment house, usually in poor condition.

Tory party: A British political party known for its conservative ideas; its modern successor is the Conservative party.

vaccine: A substance made of dead or live germs of a disease, which is given to people (or animals) to protect them against that disease.

Whig party: A British political party known for its progressive ideas; its modern successor is the Liberal party.

For Further Reading

Chiflet, Jean-Loup, and Alain Beaulet. *Victoria and Her Times.* New York: Henry Holt, 1996.

Evans, David. *How We Used To Live: Victorians Early & Late.* New York: Talman, 1991.

Shearman, Deirdre. *Queen Victoria.* New York: Chelsea House, 1986.

Wilson, Laura. *Daily Life in a Victorian House.* London: Breslich & Foss, 1993.

Young, Lesley. *Queen Victoria.* Trafalgar, England: Evans Bros., 1991.

ON-LINE INFORMATION*

http://www.applebutter.freeservers.com/worker#sadler
   Full text of the parliamentary investigations into working conditions and child labor in England in 1831 to 1832.
http://www.barnardf.demon.co.uk/
   Several letters written by Ada E. Leslie, governess to two of Queen Victoria's grandchildren.
http://www.history-magazine.com/dinner.html
   Sample recipes and other aspects of Victorian life.
http://www.history.rochester.edu/ehp-book/yethas
   The text of a book of Victorian etiquette, *Youth's Educator for Home and Society.*
http://www.housemouse.net/hkitch6.htm#recipies
   Victorian recipes and household information.

*Websites change from time to time. If you cannot find what you are looking for, use a search engine and type in a keyword. Or check with the media specialist at your local library.

Bibliography

Cannon, John, and Ralph Griffiths. *The Oxford Illustrated History of the British Monarchy.* New York: Oxford University Press, 1988.

Drabble, Margaret. *For Queen and Country: Britain in the Victorian Age.* New York: Clarion Books, 1979.

Duff, David. *Punch on Children: A Panorama 1845–1865.* London: Frederick Muller, 1975.

Hall, Unity. *The Private Lives of Britain's Royal Women.* Chicago: Contemporary Books, 1990.

Longford, Elizabeth. *Victoria R. I.* London: Pan Books, 1983.

Mountbatten-Windsor, Sarah (Duchess of York), with Benita Stoney. *Victoria and Albert: A Family Life at Osborne House.* New York: Prentice Hall, 1991.

Nevill, Barry St. John, ed. *Life at the Court of Queen Victoria, 1861–1901.* Exeter, England: Webb & Bower, 1984.

Oxford Dictionary of Quotations. 3rd ed. New York: Oxford University Press, 1979.

Paz, D. G. "Victoria." In *Historic World Leaders.* Vol. 3. Detroit: Gale Research, 1994.

Pool, Daniel. *What Jane Austen Ate and Charles Dickens Knew.* New York: Touchstone, 1993.

Stevenson, Robert Louis. *A Child's Garden of Verses.* New York: Grosset & Dunlap, 1957.

Strachey, Lytton. *Queen Victoria.* New York: Harcourt Brace, 1921.

Thompson, Dorothy. *Queen Victoria: Gender & Power.* London: Virago Press, 1990.

Victoria, Queen (of Great Britain). *Advice to My Grand-daughter: Letters from Queen Victoria to Princess Victoria of Hesse.* New York: Simon and Schuster, 1975.

Woodham-Smith, Cecil. *Queen Victoria: From Her Birth to the Death of the Prince Consort.* New York: Knopf, 1972.

Notes

Part One: England in the Victorian Age

Page 11. "Take care of her": Woodham-Smith, *Queen Victoria*, p. 32.
Page 13. "We lived in a very simple plain manner": Woodham-Smith, *Queen Victoria*, p. 55.
Page 14. "I see I am nearer to the Throne": Woodham-Smith, *Queen Victoria*, p. 76.
Page 14. "This Book Mamma gave me": Woodham-Smith, *Queen Victoria*, p. 88.
Page 15. "The men, women, children, country and houses": Woodham-Smith, *Queen Victoria*, p. 88.

Page 15. "The business of the highest in a State": Strachey, *Queen Victoria*, p. 66.

Page 15. "I was awoke at 6 o'clock": Woodham-Smith, *Queen Victoria*, p. 138.

Page 16. "Of COURSE, quite ALONE": Woodham-Smith, *Queen Victoria*, p. 139.

Page 16. "She bowed to the Lords": Cannon and Griffiths, *Oxford Illustrated History of the British Monarchy*, p. 551.

Page 17. "I have so many communications": Strachey, *Queen Victoria*, p. 92.

Page 19. "cold, unfeeling": Woodham-Smith, *Queen Victoria*, p. 172.

Page 20. "disgusted with everything": Woodham-Smith, *Queen Victoria*, p. 181.

Page 21. "Oh, when I look in those lovely, lovely blue eyes": Drabble, *For Queen and Country*, p. 17.

Page 22. "I sent for Albert": Cannon and Griffiths, *Oxford Illustrated History of the British Monarchy*, p. 558.

Page 22. "I am the Sovereign": Woodham-Smith, *Queen Victoria*, p. 206.

Page 26. "It was the happiest, proudest day in my life": Longford, *Victoria R. I.*, p. 226.

Page 30. "The poor fatherless baby of eight months": Strachey, *Queen Victoria*, pp. 302–303.

Page 33. "mad, wicked folly": Strachey, *Queen Victoria*, p. 409.

Page 34. "We are not interested in the possibilities of defeat": Cannon and Griffiths, *Oxford Illustrated History of the British Monarchy*, p. 577.

Page 35. "We all feel a bit motherless today": Cannon and Griffiths, *Oxford Illustrated History of the British Monarchy*, p. 578.

Page 35. "indifferent to": Drabble, *For Queen and Country*, p. 26.

Part Two: Everyday Life in Victorian England

Page 62. "two nations who are as ignorant of each other's habits": *Oxford Dictionary of Quotations*, p. 186.

Part Three: The Victorians in Their Own Words

Page 76. "Faster than fairies, faster than witches": Stevenson, Robert Louis, *Child's Garden of Verses*, p. 53.

Page 77. "Start in Life!": *Punch Magazine*, January 13, 1894, at http://www.library.yale.edu/~mpowell/victorianper.html#hw

Page 78. "More than a hundred thousand souls": London *Times*, September 17, 1847, at http://www3.nb.sympatico.ca/rmcusack/Story-40.html

Page 80. "Many and deep are the wounds": Whyte, Robert, *Famine Ship Diary*, at http://www.people.Virginia.EDU/~eas5e/Irish/RWhyte.html

Page 84. "A rude, loud-spoken, uncultured woman": *Youth's Educator for Home and Society*, at http://www.history.rochester.edu/ehp-book/yethas

Page 85. "Pour four quarts of boiling water": "1860's Victorian Recipies" at http://www.housemouse.net/hkitch6.htm#recipies

Page 86. "Ingredients: Haunch of mutton": Beeton, Isabella, *Book of Household Management*, 1860, at http://www.history-magazine.com/dinner.html

Page 87. "What was your business in the mill?": Parliamentary Papers, vol. XV, at http://www.applebutter.freeservers.com/worker#sadler

Index

Page numbers for illustrations are in **boldface**

packmen, 55
Parliament, 4, 17, 30
Pasteur, Louis, 68, **69**
Peel, Robert, 19, 24, 45, 89
Piccadilly Circus, 36
piemen, 56
police force, 45, 89
poor. *See* lower class
potato famine, 29, 77–79, 89
prime minister, 6–7
primogeniture, 54
Punch, 76–77

railroads, 41, 76, 89
rat catcher, 56
rat terrier, 56
recipes, 85–86
Reform Acts, 32
religion, 70
Royal Titles Act, 32

schools, 64. *See also* education
Scotland, 8
Second Reform Act, 26
servants, 50–51, **50**, **51**, 55
social inequities, 10, 46, 51, 54–55, **55**, 57–58, 86–88, **88**
steam engine, 10, 38, 39

steam hammer, **39**

telegraph, 41
telephone, 10, 41
textile mill, **55**
theory of evolution, 70
tin can, 10
Tory party, 19, 24
transportation, 41

United Kingdom. *See* Great Britain
upper class, 17, 46, 50, 52, 54, 59, **60**

Victoria, 1, 5, 6–7, 18, 23, 33
childhood, 4, 11–15, 12
children of, 22–23
correspondence with Leopold, 15, 26, 30
diary of, 14–15, 15, 16, 17, 22
evaluation of, 35
independence of, 16
marriage of, 21–22
mourning for Albert, 30, 31
preparing to be queen, 14–15

traditional values of, 5, 35
work of, 17, 22, 24, 35
Victoria (daughter), 23
Victoria Cross, 27
Victoria Mary Louisa of Saxe-Coburg (duchess of Kent), 11, **12**, 13, 15, 17, 30
Victorian Age, 5
voting privileges, 17–19, 33

Wales, 8
watermen, 56
Whig party, 19, 24
Whyte, Robert, 79
wig makers, **63**
William, 11, 13, 14
women, 89
voting and, 32–33
work and, 54
work, 54–58, **55**, **56**, 86–88, **88**
child labor, 57–58, **57**, 86–88
jobs, 55–57
laws, 26
wages, 58
working class. *See* lower class
writing, 54